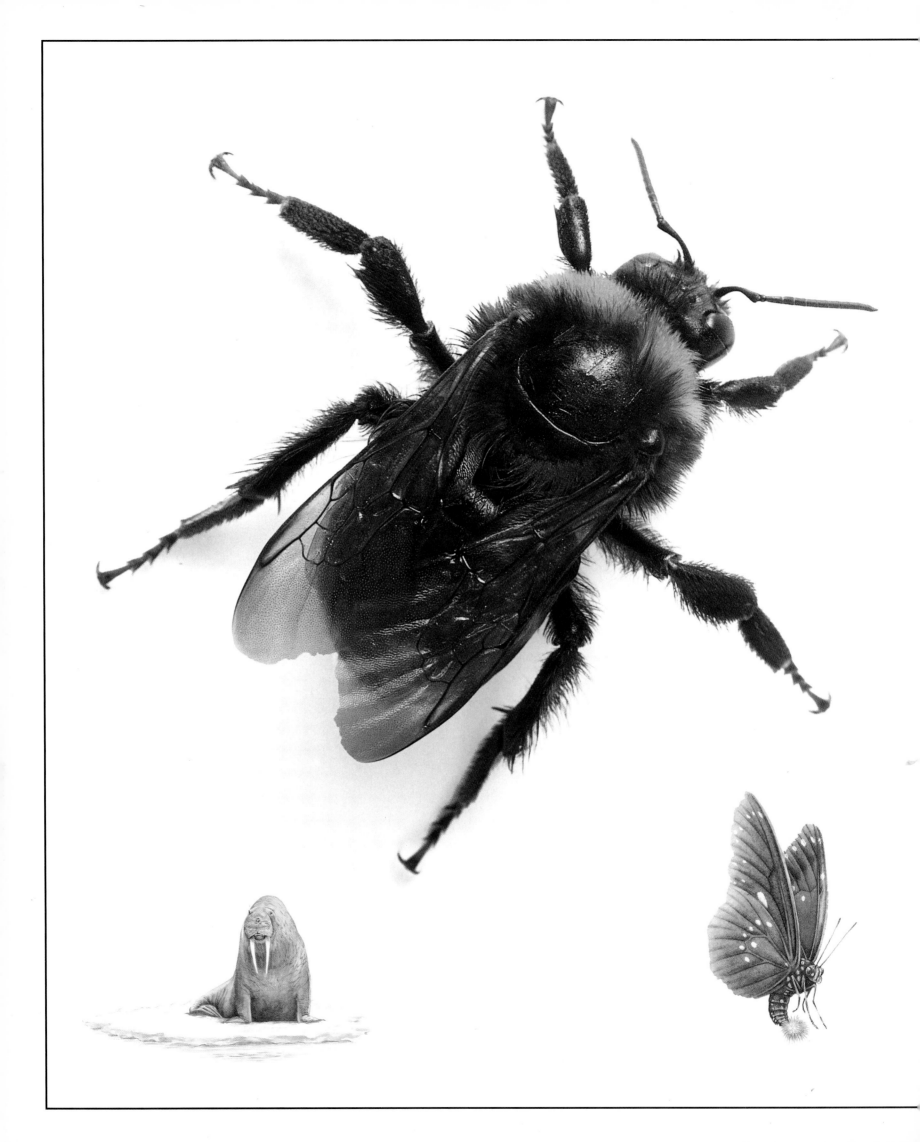

Amazing Animal Facts

WRITTEN BY
CHRISTOPHER MAYNARD

ALFRED A. KNOPF • NEW YORK

A DORLING KINDERSLEY BOOK

Editor Deborah Murrell
Art Editor Hans Verkroost
Assistant Editor Claire Bampton
Assistant Designer Susan St. Louis
Managing Editor Sophie Mitchell
Managing Art Editor Miranda Kennedy
Production Paola Fagherazzi

Additional editorial assistance
Michèle Lynch and Jane Parker

This is a Borzoi Book published by Alfred A. Knopf, Inc.

First American edition, 1993

Manufactured in Italy
10 9 8 7 6 5 4 3 2 1

Library of Congress Cataloging-in-Publication Data
Maynard, Christopher.
  Amazing animal facts : a question and answer book / written by
Christopher Maynard. – 1st American ed.
    p. cm.
  Includes index.
  Summary: Provides answers to questions about animals, including
"Where do butterflies sleep?" "Is a crayfish a fish?"
"When does a fox use a brush?" "Do crocodiles cry?"
  1. Animals–Miscellanea–Juvenile literature. [1. Animals–
Miscellanea. 2. Questions and answers.] I. Title.
QL49. M475 1993
591–dc20   93-855
ISBN 0-679-85085-6

Color reproduction by Colourscan, Singapore
Printed and bound in Italy by Graphicom, Vicenza

Contents

What do bears eat?

BEARS EAT ALMOST ANYTHING, including fruit, nuts, leaves, and insects. But fish, meat, and picnic leftovers will do nicely, and a snack of honey is something no bear can resist.

Where does the grizzly get its name?

From the white tips on the bear's fur, which make it look "grizzled," or speckled with gray.

When do cubs scout?

These black bear cubs are four months old. They have already begun to scout around outside their den, but they still rely on their mother to find food. They will leave home when they are about two years old.

Bears will fight fiercely to defend their homes.

Brown bears, like this grizzly, have long claws on their front paws.

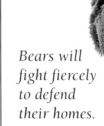

Do bears wear glasses?

The spectacled bear looks as if it does. It got its name because the dark fur around its eyes looks like eyeglasses, which people used to call spectacles.

How heavy are bears?

The heaviest brown bear is the Kodiak bear, from Alaska. A large male can tip the scales at over 1,300 pounds (600 kg). But polar bears, which live in the Arctic, are even bigger. An adult male can weigh 1,600 pounds (720 kg).

What bugs bugs?

The little sun bear from Southeast Asia – it keeps eating them! When it finds a big mound of delicious termites, it tears open the mound with its long claws and lets the termites swarm all over its paws. Then the sun bear slurps them up, dozens at a time.

BEAR FACTS

- Black bears can gallop at a speed of 30 miles per hour (50 km/h). They can also climb up trees to get out of danger.

- Bears are usually shy, but some black bears raid garbage dumps, trash cans, and even backyard bird feeders!

- Polar bears can grow to 8 feet (2.5 m) from their head to their tail.

- Teddy bears are named after President Teddy Roosevelt, who became very popular after he refused to shoot a bear cub in 1902.

When is it good to have a stuffed nose?

When you're a sloth bear. This animal (below) pokes its long snout into termite nests to suck up the insects. Fortunately, a sloth bear can close its nostrils to stop itchy termites from crawling up its nose.

DID YOU KNOW?
The panda (below) feeds on bamboo, a tall, tough grass with little nutrition. An adult panda has to eat about 45 pounds (20 kg) of bamboo stems a day.

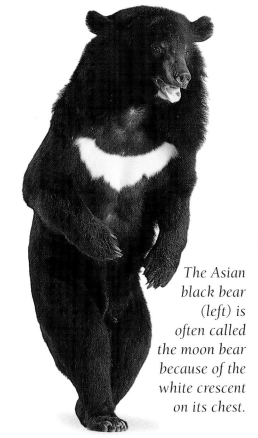

The Asian black bear (left) is often called the moon bear because of the white crescent on its chest.

Can bears dance?

All bears can stand and walk on their hind legs. Asian black bears, like the one above, can balance on two feet almost as well as you can. Sadly, this has tempted some people to catch black bear cubs and train them to dance in circuses and carnivals.

How do bears talk?

Bears use body language to communicate, as well as growls and grunts. A direct stare is a warning, and a bear with its head lowered is about to attack.

What keeps a polar bear warm?

Polar bears have a thick layer of fat under their skin to keep heat in as they hunt for food in the icy Arctic Ocean. A polar bear can get so hot lying in the sun that it will jump into the sea just to cool off.

DID YOU KNOW?
Male bears scratch marks on trees to warn off other bears. The higher the mark, the bigger the bear.

Are some dogs wild?

MOST OF THE DOGS WE KEEP as pets would not survive without us to feed them. But all dogs are related to wolves. Wolves probably once hunted with people and then moved into their homes, gradually changing into the pet dogs we have today. There are still more than thirty kinds of wild dogs, including coyotes, jackals, and dingoes.

What do wild puppies eat?

Adult wild dogs have to hunt food for their pups. Often the adults chew the meat first to make it easier for the pups to eat with their tiny teeth.

Can dogs fight wars?

The ancestors of the Bernese mountain dog (below) pulled carts for Roman soldiers. And 4,000 years ago, people in the Middle East kept similar dogs for hunting and fighting.

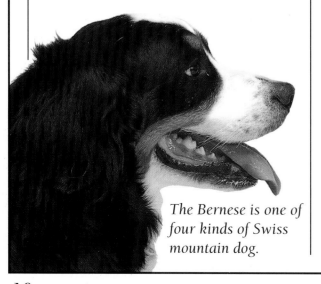

The Bernese is one of four kinds of Swiss mountain dog.

Are toy dogs real?

Yes, they are. They get their name because of their size. Pekingese dogs (above) were once the sacred pets of the emperor of China. People had to bow before them, and the punishment for stealing a Pekingese was death.

Why do dogs live in packs?

Most wild dogs hunt, rest, and travel in groups called packs. This way of life makes good sense. The adults can protect the young pups; and by hunting as a pack, dogs can kill animals larger than they could ever manage to on their own.

What is a hyena?

A hyena (above) may look like a dog, but it is more closely related to weasels and cats. Hyenas probably look like dogs because they live in similar places and hunt the same kinds of prey.

German shepherds are often used as guide dogs by blind people.

Which dog is most like a wolf?

People have bred German shepherd dogs to look as much like wolves as possible. But their behavior is no more wolflike than any other dog's.

Can dogs do tricks?

Some dogs can. The Bichon Frisé (above) was once popular among French nobles. But after the French Revolution in 1789, when the king and nobility were overthrown, many of these dogs were taken into circuses and trained to perform tricks.

Do bush dogs live in bushes?

No, but they do live among bushes. A short tail and a small, thick body make it easy for the bush dog to move about in the undergrowth, as well as in its underground home.

Bush dogs

How many dogs make a pack?

African wild dogs working in packs of ten or twenty can hunt animals as large as antelopes or wildebeest. The leader grabs the prey to slow it down, then the rest mob it and drag it to the ground.

What are firehouse dogs?

The dalmatian was once popular as a fire-station mascot, or "firehouse dog." Until cars became common at the beginning of this century, dalmatians also served as coach dogs, trotting by the wheels of carriages.

By hunting in packs, the African wild dog makes up for its small size.

DOG FACTS

- Dogs have much better hearing than human beings. Wild dogs can hear a ticking watch from 30 feet (100 m) away.

- A coyote howls to warn other coyotes to stay out of its territory. It often finds a high place to howl from so the sound can be heard over a larger area.

- Dogs can't retract (pull in) their claws as cats can, so you can always see the shape of the claws in a dog's paw prints.

- A dog can build up a mental picture of another dog using only its sense of smell.

Do all dogs hunt?

All wild dogs hunt, but most pet dogs would starve if they were left to fend for themselves. Some breeds, though, like this tough bull terrier, still have a powerful instinct for hunting.

What do foxes eat?

YOUR LEFTOVERS, SOMETIMES. They often make their way across fields or along overgrown railroad tracks at night, to feed on the food that people throw into their trash cans.

Can foxes climb?

Most foxes are happiest on the ground. But the gray fox (below) has an unusual ability – it can scamper up and down tree trunks. It grips the bark with its front paws and pushes itself up with its back legs.

The Arctic fox seldom needs to do its own hunting.

Where do Arctic foxes find food?

Arctic foxes are happy to eat a polar bear's leftovers. A fox will sometimes trail along after a bear and live on its scraps.

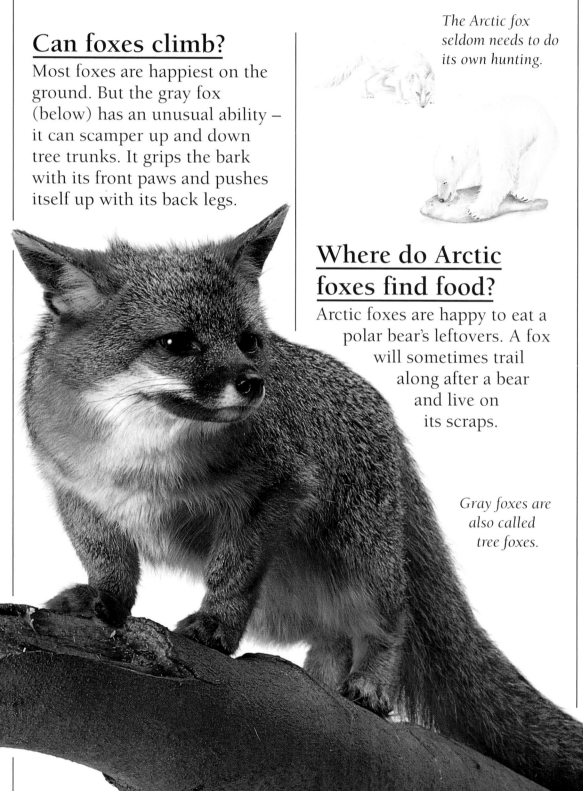

Gray foxes are also called tree foxes.

What can a fox hear?

This bat-eared fox's large ears pick up sounds that we could never hear. The fox needs good hearing to find the insects that it feeds on.

When do foxes pounce?

When they get close to a small animal, such as a mouse, foxes often leap into the air and pounce on it with both front paws, pinning the animal to the ground.

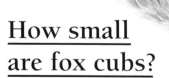

How small are fox cubs?

Fox cubs are tiny at birth. They weigh about 3.5 ounces (100 g) and are no bigger than a mouse. They are blind and totally dependent on their mother.

There are four kinds of desert foxes. They hide in the shadows of rocks for much of the day. All four kinds have large ears, which give off heat easily and help keep the foxes cool.

When do foxes change their coats?

The Arctic fox (above) has a white winter coat that hides it against the snow. In spring the white fur falls out and the fox grows a brown summer coat.

How small are foxes?

The fennec fox (above) is one of the smallest foxes, with a body about 16 inches (40 cm) long. It lives in the Sahara Desert in Africa and feeds on insects.

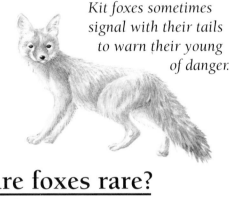

Kit foxes sometimes signal with their tails to warn their young of danger.

Are foxes rare?

Kit foxes are. Once they were quite common, but because people have destroyed most of their habitat, only about 7,000 are left today.

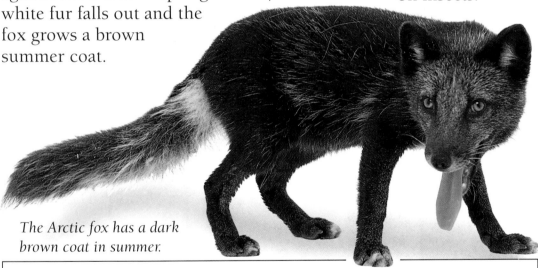

The Arctic fox has a dark brown coat in summer.

FOX FACTS

- Foxes eat small animals, such as frogs, birds, and insects. When prey is hard to find, they will eat berries and fruits.

- A female fox is called a vixen, and her underground home is called an earth.

- The pads on a desert fox's paws are covered with fur, for protection against hot rocks and sand.

The Arctic fox has a dark brown coat in summer.

When does a fox use a brush?

A brush is the name for a fox's tail. It is long, thick, and bushy, so it makes a cozy blanket in cold weather. The fox wraps its tail around its paws and face to keep warm.

Is a wolf a dog?

WOLVES ARE THE LARGEST members of the dog family. They grow to be 3 feet (1 m) tall at the shoulder and can weigh as much as 110 pounds (50 kg). When there is enough food, wolves live in packs of up to twenty members.

Can wolves sing?

No, but they can howl loudly! All the wolves in a pack, including the cubs, howl to keep in touch when separated and to warn other wolves away.

Do wolves attack people?

Not unless they think the person might hurt them or their young. Most stories of wolves attacking people are untrue.

Which wolf isn't a wolf at all?

The maned wolf (above) has long legs, like a wolf. But it has bigger ears and a lighter body than a wolf. It is actually a wild dog that lives only in South America.

Do wolves speak?

No, but they communicate very well with their face and body as well as their voice. Animals that live in packs must know who the leader is and obey his commands.

Why do wolves make trails?

Wolves leave trails of scent on trees, bushes, and rocks to warn off other wolves. A strange wolf entering another pack's territory will be chased away – sometimes even killed.

Do Arctic wolves eat Arctic hares?

The Arctic wolf usually feeds on caribou, or reindeer, but when food is scarce, it will take whatever it can get. An Arctic hare makes a perfectly good meal for a hungry wolf.

What color is a gray wolf?

Despite its name, the gray wolf's coat is not always gray. It can be black, cream, brown, or a mixture of colors. Often, the coat is similar in color to the wolf's surroundings, for camouflage (disguise).

The Arctic wolf (below) is a kind of gray wolf. Its coat turns almost white in winter.

A wolf's strong legs are good for running long distances.

How fast are wolves?

Wolves run fast only in short bursts. What they are best at is slow running, called loping. A pack often trails its prey in this way for hours, until the animal is so tired it can't run anymore.

How many kinds of wolf are there?

Many kinds of dogs are called wolves, including the prairie wolf, or coyote. But the gray wolf, also called the timber wolf, and the red wolf are the only true kinds.

Do cubs hunt?

This wolf cub is much too small to hunt with the rest of the pack. It will not go scouting for food with the adults until it is about six months old.

WOLF FACTS

- Wolf cubs live on their mother's milk for the first few weeks of their lives, just like human babies.

- Wolves can reach speeds of up to 40 miles per hour (65 km/h) in short bursts. They can also keep up a steady pace for many hours covering vast distances.

- When a mother goes hunting, the father or another adult baby-sits the cubs until she returns with food.

15

Are "big cats" big?

WE USE THE WORDS "BIG CATS" to describe five species, or kinds, of wild cats – lions, tigers, jaguars, leopards, and snow leopards. And compared with domestic, or pet, cats, "big cats" are giants!

The leopard is good at climbing trees. Its long tail helps it to balance.

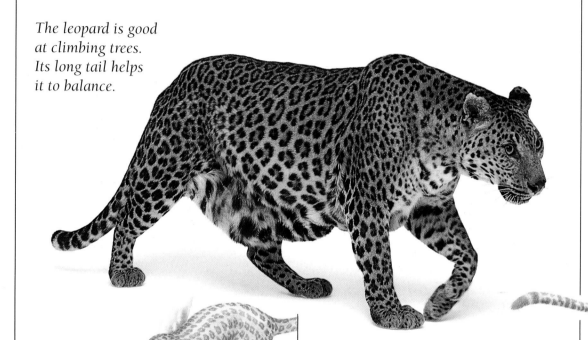

Do cats like water?

Some do. Tigers are strong swimmers. They often wade into water to cool off, and sometimes catch frogs and fish to snack on.

How fast are cats?

The cheetah is the fastest land animal. It can run at 70 miles per hour (90 km/h), but only for a short distance, and only in a straight line. A fast antelope can often escape a cheetah.

Are spots useful?

Leopards are covered in spots. These markings help leopards hide against the background, but they also lead to their death because people kill the leopards and use their skin for fur coats.

DID YOU KNOW?
Neither the cheetah (above) nor the caracal (below) are "big cats," but they are not very small, either. The caracal lives in the desert and hunts in the cool of the night for hares, lizards, and other animals. It can jump so high and fast that it can catch birds as they fly past.

When do leopards hunt?

Leopards spend the day lazing around in the branches of trees. When evening comes, they climb down and set off alone to hunt. Sometimes they simply lie in wait on a branch and pounce on an antelope or other animal passing below.

How do lions roar?

The voice box of a big cat, unlike most cats, is joined to its skull. This is what gives the cat its loud roar. But when a big cat purrs, it has to pause for breath every so often. Small cats can purr nonstop, but they can't roar.

Lions are the only cats that live in family groups, called prides.

Can a leopard change its spots?

Not whenever it chooses, but there is a kind of leopard whose spots are so faded that they are hardly visible. This animal is known as the black panther (left), and it is most common in parts of India.

How do cats hide?

Resting in a tree, a leopard is almost invisible among the shadows. But a flick of the tail can give it away.

What do lions eat?

Almost anything they can catch, including wildebeest, zebras, and buffaloes. Female lions do most of the hard work. They hunt in teams, trying to circle their prey before it spots them. One lioness drives it toward the others, who bring it to the ground and kill it with a quick bite to the throat.

Do pumas have spots?

The puma (below) is born spotted, but after about three months the spots begin to fade. At about six months old, pumas are red-brown all over.

Puma, mountain lion, and cougar are all different names for the same cat.

"BIG CAT" FACTS

- In India, legend says leopards are so cunning that they brush away their tracks with their tails.

- The snow leopard has a white coat with dark spots. It is easy to mistake one for a snow-speckled rock if it sits very still.

- Tigers are the biggest cats of all. A large Siberian tiger can weigh over 450 pounds (200 kg).

Do small cats hunt?

THEY CERTAINLY DO. Cats are great climbers, runners, and jumpers, and that makes them good hunters. They have many more bones than humans do, and they can stretch and bend in ways that we can only dream about. They also have sharp claws for attacking and gripping prey.

Why is it hard to spot some cats?

The leopard cat (below) is a wild cat whose spotted coat makes it look like a small leopard. The spots help to hide the leopard cat from its prey.

Why do cats play with their food?

Sometimes a cat catches a mouse or a bird and plays with it instead of eating it. This play helps improve the cat's killing skills. It takes a long time for a kitten to learn how to hunt, and even adult cats have to stay in practice.

Do pets paddle?

Cats can swim, but most hate the water – except the Turkish swimming cat, which loves to paddle in shallow pools and streams. It has no thick underfur, so it dries off quickly.

Why do cats lick their paws?

To clean their fur. Cats have rough tongues that remove the dirt and brush the fur smooth. But a cat's tongue won't reach its ears, so the cat licks its paw first, and uses the wet paw to clean its ears.

What is a tail for?

A tail helps a cat balance. As the cat launches itself into the air, it flicks its tail straight up, then holds it stiffly until it lands safely on the ground.

When a cat jumps, it pushes off with its long back legs, stretches out full length, and lands on its short, strong front legs.

Do cats have nine lives?

Of course not – this saying began because cats are so good at surviving a fall. They twist their bodies in midair and usually land safely on their feet.

SMALL CAT FACTS

- When an Abyssinian cat meows, it sounds more like a bird singing.

- The smallest wild cat is the rusty-spotted cat of India. It usually weighs less than 3 pounds (1.5 kg).

- A cat's eyes glow in the dark because a special layer at the back of the eye reflects light like a mirror.

DID YOU KNOW?
Cats eat grass to help them cough up fur they swallowed during grooming.

Are black cats lucky?

In America a black cat crossing your path is thought to bring bad luck. In other countries a black cat is a sign of good luck.

Why do cats arch their backs?

Pet cats purr when they are happy and hiss when they are angry. A frightened cat arches its back and raises its fur on end to make itself look bigger to its enemy.

What is a bobcat?

A bobcat is a medium-sized North American wild cat. It has a short, "bobbed" (clipped) tail, tufted ears, and a ruff of fur behind the head. Bobcats hunt at night for rabbits and birds.

Are bats birds?

BECAUSE BATS HAVE WINGS and can fly well, they look a bit like birds. But they are really mammals. There are more than 1,000 kinds of bats. They live in tropical rain forests, woods, caves, and towns.

Bats often roost, or rest, together in a cave during the day.

Why do bats sleep upside down?

Because it's comfortable. Bats have to sleep this way because their legs are not strong enough to stand, and they cannot grip with their hands. The only way they can relax enough to sleep is by hanging upside down, holding on with their feet.

Do bats drink blood?

Only the vampire bat (above) has a taste for blood. It lives in parts of Central and South America and feeds at night on the blood of sleeping horses and cattle. Most other kinds of bats live on insects, fruit, or nectar. And a few bats eat fish!

Do bats have hands?

Bats' hands are actually wings, with a sheet of thin skin stretched between very long finger bones.

DID YOU KNOW?
In summer, bats often get too hot. So they find a cool, dark place to rest in, such as a closet or a cupboard. You could find a bat inside your clothes!

How blind is a bat?

People often use the phrase "as blind as a bat." In fact, bats are not blind at all. They can see perfectly well in daylight. But at night, their eyesight is just like yours – not very good!

Bats use their tails for balance.

Do bats take their babies to nurseries?

Female bats have only two or three babies a year, but they all have them at the same time. They take care of the babies in large groups, called nurseries. Some nurseries can contain up to a million babies.

DID YOU KNOW?
Female bats with no young of their own often join a nursery and help other females care for their young.

Do bats make tents?

There is a bat in Central America that makes tents. This tiny fruit-eating bat (below) bites along the strong rib in the middle of a palm leaf so that the sides fold down over the bat like a tent.

These bats hang on to the leaf by tucking their feet through the holes they have made.

When does a bat have a ball?

When it finds a cloud of insects in the dark! When they hunt at night, many bats use a trick called echolocation to find food – and to keep from bumping into things! As the bat flies along, it makes high-pitched squeaks. When the squeaks hit an insect, they bounce back. The bat hears the echo and finds the insect.

What do bats do in winter?

Some bats live in places where there is no food for them in winter. They choose a quiet shelter, such as a hollow tree or a cave, where they fall into a deep sleep, called hibernation. A hibernating bat breathes so slowly that it is hard to tell whether it is alive or dead.

Hibernating close together helps bats keep from losing too much moisture.

A bat's wings need to be kept in good condition for flying.

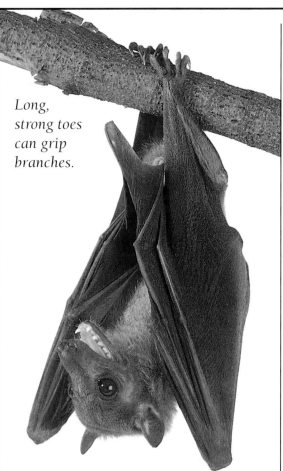

Long, strong toes can grip branches.

When is a bat a fox?

When it's a flying fox (above). Some fruit bats are called flying foxes because of their ginger-colored fur, large brown eyes, and pointed, foxlike noses.

DID YOU KNOW? This bulldog bat goes fishing using the special hooks on its back legs.

BAT FACTS

- The largest bats are flying foxes. Some have a wingspan of more than 3 feet (1 m).

- Young bats can usually fly by the time they are four months old.

- The smallest bat, the bumblebee bat, is only 1 inch (3 cm) long – about the size of your big toe.

- The only bat that can walk along the ground is the vampire bat.

Are apes like us?

APES AND MONKEYS ARE more closely related to humans than any other animal. You can see this in their faces and hands. They often chatter and play games, and there's nothing more human than that!

When do baboons mate?

The red, swollen area under the tail of this female hamadryas baboon is a clear sign that she is at her most fertile. If she mates now, there is a good chance that she will produce young.

How good is a gibbon's balance?

Very good indeed – even a female with her young can travel quickly through the forest, running along branches like a tightrope walker.

What is a primate?

Primates are mammals that live in trees and, in some cases, on the ground as well. Apes, lemurs, and gorillas are primates. The most common primates are human beings.

Where do lemurs live?

Lemurs are small primates that live only on Madagascar, an island off Southeast Africa. The aye-aye (above), which is almost extinct, is a small, bushy-tailed kind of lemur.

The De Brazza's monkey's long tail helps it to balance in trees.

MONKEY FACTS

- Just like people, monkeys live in families. A big troop, or group, might contain as many as fifty monkeys.

- Gibbons and humans are the only primates that can walk comfortably on their hind legs.

- The biggest primate of all is the gorilla. It weighs 3,000 times as much as the gray mouse lemur, which is the smallest primate.

22

Which animal is named after us?

The orangutan (left) looks so much like us that people formed its name from the Malay words for "man" and "forest."

This owl monkey can see so well in the dark that it can catch insects as they fly past.

What makes a monkey attractive?

In the case of the proboscis monkey (below), it is the large nose, or proboscis. In the breeding season the male with the largest nose is the one most females choose to mate with.

When do monkeys get a grip?

Monkeys can grip when they are born. It is often up to the baby to hold on to an adult as tightly as it can, like this golden lion tamarin clinging to his mother's fur.

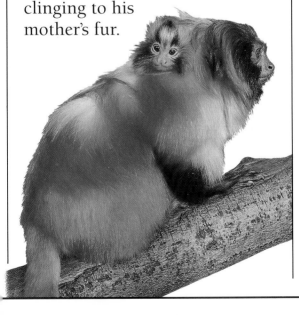

What do monkeys do at night?

Most monkeys curl up and go to sleep at night. But the owl monkey goes hunting. It gets its name from its huge eyes and owllike hoot.

Tails that grasp like this are called prehensile tails.

Do monkeys have five arms?

No, but many monkeys, like the spider monkey (above), use the tail like an extra arm. This way they can hang from a branch and still have their hands free for eating.

Can monkeys learn new tricks?

All monkeys are fast learners, but macaques are especially clever. They pick up tricks from each other very quickly. A crab-eating macaque (above) learns from its parents how to fish for crabs and how to get the meat out of the shell.

Chimps make and use tools, just as we do.

Are chimps smart?

Chimpanzees are among the smartest animals in the world. They even make tools by ripping the leaves off thin sticks and poking them into anthills to draw out ants.

What are mammals?

MAMMALS ARE WARM-BLOODED ANIMALS. They give birth to live young, which feed on their mother's milk. Elephants, whales, and porcupines are mammals; humans and apes are too.

Why do gorillas beat their chests?

To settle an argument. Two males will roar, bark, tear up leaves, and beat their chests. The smaller gorilla usually backs down before a real fight begins.

How do walruses keep from freezing?

Under its skin the walrus has a layer of thick fat called blubber. It helps keep out the Arctic cold.

The ears of an Indian elephant are smaller than an African elephant's.

The elephant's huge feet spread out and keep it from sinking into soft ground.

Are mammals large?

Some are. The elephant is the largest land animal, but the ocean-dwelling blue whale is many times bigger. A female can grow to be 100 feet (33 m) long. Blue whales eat about four tons of tiny, shrimplike creatures called krill a day.

The blue whale is the loudest animal as well as the biggest.

How do elephants keep cool?

By using their ears. Elephants live in the hottest parts of Africa and India, and their huge ears give off heat and help them stay cool. They can also flap their ears like fans.

There are about 60,000 muscles in an elephant's trunk.

How does an elephant smell?

With its trunk. But an elephant also uses its trunk to put food into its mouth, suck up and squirt water for washing and drinking, and call to other elephants.

Does a camel have one hump or two?

Dromedaries, or Arabian camels, have one hump. Bactrian camels, like this one, have two.

Are rhinoceroses thick-skinned?

Very. Their skin protects them from other animals. Insects cannot bite or sting through a rhino's skin, and even the sharp claws of a big cat cannot grip it.

Why do musk oxen make circles?

To protect their young. If wolves come near, the adults form a circle around the young. No matter where a wolf attacks, it always faces a set of horns.

DID YOU KNOW?
The hippopotamus gets its name from the ancient Greek words for "river" and "horse."

A giraffe calf is about 6 feet (2 m) tall when it is born – but it still has to reach up to its mother for milk.

Why do mammals drink milk?

Mammals are too weak to feed themselves when they are born, so their mothers provide them with milk. A mother's milk is very nutritious, and contains everything a baby needs.

When do pandas climb trees?

When they are tired. Pandas sleep a lot to save energy. Often they climb a tree and wedge themselves into a comfortable notch in the branches. Here they are safe from enemies – and from falling out of the tree!

Rhinos are famous for their bad tempers. The only animal that dares to attack them is a human with a gun.

MAMMAL FACTS

- The bumblebee bat is the smallest mammal in the world. It is less than 1/1000 the length of a blue whale.

- The only egg-laying mammals alive today are the platypus and the echidna. All other mammals give birth to live young.

- Human babies develop inside their mother for nine months. Elephant babies develop for 22 months, longer than any other mammal.

What are shells for?

AN ANIMAL'S SHELL usually protects the soft parts of its body. The largest group of animals with shells is the mollusk group, which includes snails, clams, mussels, and whelks.

Why do scallops clap?

Because that's how they swim. When a scallop (below) is alarmed, it claps the two halves of its shell together. Water shoots out in one direction, and the scallop scoots off in another.

How do snails make shells?

The pond snail (left) lives in water that has lots of chalk. The snail uses the chalk to build its shell. As its body grows, it adds to the open end of the shell to make it bigger.

Giant clams get much of their food from tiny, simple plants called algae.

How much can mollusks weigh?

The giant clam (right) is the biggest mollusk in the world. It can weigh more than two adult humans. The part of the clam's skin that builds the shell is called the mantle.

Are shells dangerous?

Cone shells are among the most beautiful shells in the world. But the animals inside them are deadly. They shoot a poison dart into their prey to paralyze it. The poison of one kind of cone shell is strong enough to kill a person.

Do snails form bands?

The European striped snail makes a shell with regular bands all around it. The bands are usually similar in color to the snail's habitat and help it to blend in with its surroundings.

What if you get too big for your shell?

When the nautilus (below) grows too big for its shell, it moves but doesn't leave home. It just builds a bigger chamber, seals off the old one, and moves into the new one. The old chambers fill with air and help the nautilus to float.

This apple snail has been specially bred by people for its beautiful yellow shell.

Can a whelk walk?

The whelk (above) is a small, marine (sea-living) snail that lives just below the tide line. Whelks have a single large foot containing muscles that move in waves to push the animal slowly along.

What lays its eggs in a cloud?

Once a year, giant clams release a cloud of billions of eggs into the water. Most of the eggs will not be fertilized, and of those that are, most will be eaten.

Do snails have hands?

No, but they are often called left-handed or right-handed. Most snail shells coil in a clockwise direction. These are right-handed shells. Those that coil counter-clockwise are left-handed.

An octopus can change color to match its background in seconds, so it can hide almost anywhere.

Are slugs plants?

Many sea slugs look like bright, frilly plants. In fact, they are related to snails, although they don't have outer shells. They are protected by their nasty taste, and their bright colors warn enemies that they are not good to eat.

Does an octopus use its arms to swim?

An octopus's arms are for clinging to rocks and walking slowly along the sea bed. In order to move fast, it swims using jet propulsion. It squirts jets of water out of its siphon and shoots off backward.

Can a snail shut its shell?

Many snails have a tough disk called an operculum on their foot. The snail can pull the operculum up to block the opening of its shell and protect its soft body.

MOLLUSK FACTS

• Squid and cuttlefish are mollusks, but their shells are inside their bodies. And an octopus is a mollusk with no shell at all.

• Most water snails have heavier shells than land snails. But they can still move because the water supports some of the weight.

• The giant land snail lays eggs about 1 inch (2.5 cm) wide. People sometimes mistake them for birds' eggs.

Who needs knees?

YOU DO, AND SO DO SPIDERS. Spiders have eight legs, and each leg has six joints. That's like having 48 knees. With all those joints it's not surprising that spiders can wave their legs in almost any direction.

The Chilean red-leg spider is so big it sometimes feeds on mice and birds.

Which spider has the hairiest legs?

The Chilean red-leg is one of the hairiest spiders in the world. It has eight eyes, but none of them can see well. So it uses the long hairs on its legs as feelers to find its way around.

Do spiders shut doors?

Trap-door spiders shut themselves in burrows as protection from their enemies. This one plugs the entrance with its flat, hard abdomen (rear end). Others use mud, or weave doors from silk.

How do young scorpions travel?

A female scorpion carries her babies around on her back until they are about two weeks old. If one falls off, she stops and waits while it climbs back up. Female scorpions defend their young with their claws and their stings.

A scorpion's claw is a useful weapon.

Which spiders jump?

Jumping spiders like the one above pounce on their prey the way cats pounce on mice. They often spin a safety rope of silk thread, which they anchor to the ground before they leap.

DID YOU KNOW? Scorpions and spiders both belong to the group of animals called arachnids.

Although they are related, these two animals sometimes fight over food.

Do spiders have hairy escapes?

The bird-eating spider (above) does. With its back legs, it plucks hairs from its body and flicks them at an attacker. Each hair, shaped like a harpoon, makes the enemy itch and sneeze.

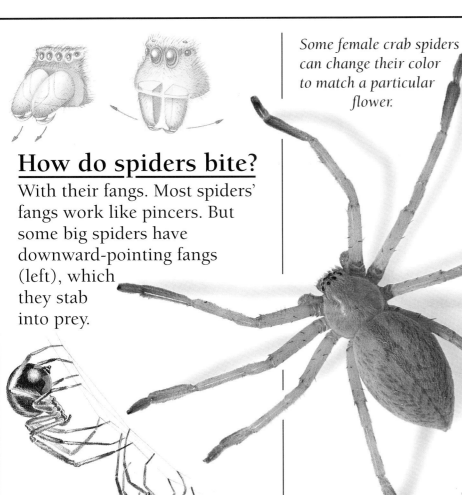

Some female crab spiders can change their color to match a particular flower.

How do spiders bite?

With their fangs. Most spiders' fangs work like pincers. But some big spiders have downward-pointing fangs (left), which they stab into prey.

Do spiders eat each other?

When the tiny male black widow spider approaches a female for mating (above), he is in danger of being eaten. So he gives her a big fresh insect wrapped in silk to eat instead.

Do spiders get caught in their own webs?

The garden spider weaves a sticky web to catch its prey. But the spider's feet are coated with oil, so it doesn't trap itself.

Changing color can take up to three days.

Do spiders like flowers?

The crab spider (above) is fond of flowers the same color as it is. The spider sits still on the petals so flying insects can't see it. When an insect lands on the flower, the spider pounces.

Can spiders kill people?

This Brazilian wandering spider is poisonous enough to kill a person. A bite from a black widow or a funnel web spider can also be deadly if an antidote is not given in time.

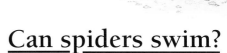

Can spiders swim?

Many spiders live near water, but only one lives under water. Like all spiders, it has to breathe air, so it spins a bell-shaped web and fills it with bubbles of air.

Water spider

SPIDER FACTS

- A spider's thread is stronger than steel of the same thickness.

- The black orb weaver uses enough silk in its web to wrap around this book 40 times.

- Some tiny spiders can travel for many miles on the wind. They spin a tangle of silk threads, which works a bit like a parachute.

- Sprays that kill most spiders just make funnel web spiders even more angry and dangerous.

29

Are beetles rare?

THERE ARE AT LEAST 350,000 different kinds of beetles. They are the most common insects. And they live nearly everywhere in the world, except in ice and snow.

Which beetles have huge snouts?

Weevils are sometimes called snout beetles because many have amazingly long snouts. Female weevils use their snouts to drill holes in plants, where they lay their eggs.

Who likes ladybugs?

Gardeners are always happy to give a home to ladybugs. Most ladybugs have a huge appetite for greenfly and blackfly, two kinds of insects that cause damage to plants.

Which beetle does nobody love?

Farmers and gardeners hate the Colorado beetle for the damage it does to potato plants. But before people introduced the potato to the U.S., these beetles fed only on wild desert plants.

DID YOU KNOW?
The larvae of the arrow poison beetle are not born poisonous. But poison from the leaves they feed on stays in their body and protects them from enemies.

Do stag beetles have antlers?

The stag beetle (above) got its name because its huge jaws look like a stag's antlers. The males use their jaws to wrestle other males in the breeding season, just as real stags do. The jaws aren't as dangerous as they look, so the beetles aren't usually hurt.

Whirligig beetles look a bit like tiny rowboats.

Can beetles swim?

Whirligigs are little beetles that skim over the surface of ponds and lakes like tiny, upturned boats, using their legs like oars. They often spin around in circles, which is what gives them their name. But nobody is quite sure why they spin.

BEETLE FACTS

- Deathwatch beetles tap messages to each other from their tunnels inside old wooden beams and floorboards.

- Some beetles live on the fur of mice. They eat the larvae of the fleas that also live there.

Deathwatch beetles

- Carpet beetles eat not only carpets but curtains, clothes, and even stuffed animals.

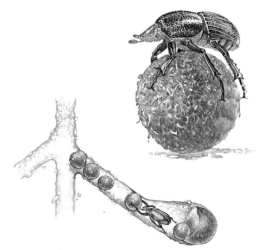

Do beetles play ball?

Dung beetles roll dung (animal droppings) into balls, just as we make snowballs. Then they roll the balls into their burrows. The females lay their eggs in the dung so the young have plenty of food when they hatch out.

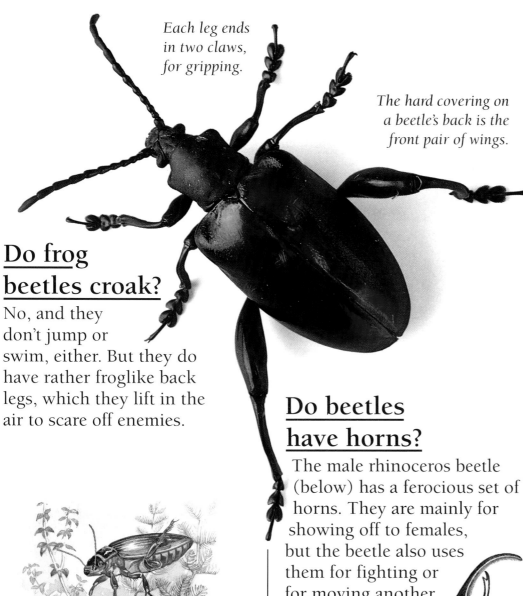

Each leg ends in two claws, for gripping.

The hard covering on a beetle's back is the front pair of wings.

Do frog beetles croak?

No, and they don't jump or swim, either. But they do have rather froglike back legs, which they lift in the air to scare off enemies.

Do beetles have horns?

The male rhinoceros beetle (below) has a ferocious set of horns. They are mainly for showing off to females, but the beetle also uses them for fighting or for moving another male beetle out of the way.

Can beetles breathe under water?

The great diving beetle can. It stores bubbles of air under its front wings and breathes the air when under water.

Are beetles pests?

Beetles can be a real nuisance at certain stages in their life. The adult longhorn beetle (above) doesn't cause much harm, but its larvae tunnel through wood and kill all kinds of trees.

Why do bees sting?

BEES STING ONLY TO DEFEND themselves or their hive. A honeybee's sting is barbed like a fishhook and usually stays in the flesh of the animal it has stung. When this happens, the bee dies, so it doesn't use its sting unless it really needs to.

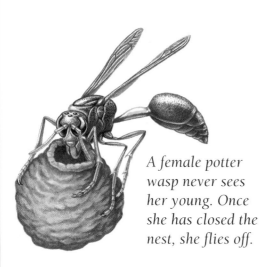

A female potter wasp never sees her young. Once she has closed the nest, she flies off.

Do wasps make pots?

Potter wasps do. Before a female lays an egg, she builds a little mud pot. Into it she places the egg and a fresh caterpillar, which the young wasp, called a larva, will eat when it hatches.

What do hunting wasps hunt?

Anything that their young can eat, such as caterpillars, beetles, and spiders. But the adults do not usually eat meat themselves – they feed mostly on fruit juice and nectar from flowers.

Are wasps sociable?

Most kinds of wasp, like this tarantula-eating wasp (below), live alone. But some, including the common wasp, build papery nests, where they live and bring up their young in groups.

Do all bees live in hives?

We often think of bees as insects that live in large groups. In fact, most of the 19,000 different kinds of bees live on their own.

What makes bees swarm?

When a new queen is born, the hive splits in two. A great swarm of bees leaves with one queen to find a new home.

A swarm often rests on a tree while a few bees go out and look for a good nesting site.

How long do bees live?

A queen honeybee may live for as long as five years. A queen bumblebee may live a few years but dies after she has raised her first colony. Worker bees are born in spring and die out in autumn.

A queen bumblebee lays several batches of eggs. The firstborn batch always hatch into workers.

How different are bees from wasps?

Wasps feed their young on insects and spiders, but bees gather nectar and pollen from flowers to feed theirs. Bees' bodies are covered in hair, but wasps usually have hairless bodies.

How do paper wasps make their nests?

Paper wasps build paper nests. They chew tree fibers into pulp, which they use to mold a nest. The pulp dries as a light but tough material.

Why do bees dance?

The pattern a bee makes in its dance describes how far away and in what direction food can be found. A circular dance means pollen and nectar can be found less than 150 feet (50 m) away. A figure-of-eight dance means the food is farther away.

How is honey made?

When a bee visits a flower, it sucks up the flower's nectar and carries it back to the hive in a special honey stomach. Other bees mix it with a liquid from their mouths and pour the mixture into the honeycomb. After about three days the liquid turns into honey.

Do wasps dig holes?

The female jewel wasp (below) digs a hole in the ground to make a nest for her egg. She moves grains of sand with her jaws and uses her legs to kick away loose bits and pieces.

BEE & WASP FACTS

- Cuckoo bees lay their eggs in the nests of other bees. This way they avoid all the hard work of running a hive.

- Honeybees visit shallow, open flowers to get nectar. Bumblebees have longer tongues, so they can go to flowers with deeper cups.

- Some tiny wasps, called chalcids, lay their eggs in the eggs of other insects. The chalcid wasp's young hatch out first and feed on the host egg.

- The yellow jackets (or hornets) you see in spring and summer make a kind of paper for their nests.

Are moths shy?

YOU DON'T SEE MOTHS AS OFTEN as you see butterflies. This is not because they are shy, but because most of them fly at night, when you are asleep. There are many more kinds of moths than butterflies.

What's hairy and tastes bad?

The tiger moth caterpillar (below) looks like a fat, hairy worm. It tastes so bad that most birds leave it alone. The only bird that eats these juicy morsels is the cuckoo.

How well do moths smell?

Moths have an amazing sense of smell. Females attract males by giving off a special perfume. A male can smell it from several miles away with its big, feathery antennae. It follows the scent directly to the female.

Can moths sting?

Moths have no stings, but some kinds fool enemies into thinking that they do. This European moth (above) is harmless. But because it looks like a hornet, which stings, other animals don't attack it.

DID YOU KNOW?
This winter moth lives only during the winter months. The female has no wings, but she doesn't need them. After emerging from her pupa – the stage between larva and adult – she only has to crawl up a tree to lay her eggs.

How do moths hide?

Moths that fly at night have to be well disguised so that they can rest safely during the day. This oleander hawk moth (above) has a pattern on its back and wings that makes it almost invisible on oleander leaves.

Do moths use straws?

Like butterflies, many moths sip nectar. They push their long, strawlike tongue, called a proboscis, to the bottom of flowers. This hawk moth has a proboscis about three times the length of its body. When it is not feeding, the moth rolls its proboscis up like a spring.

This teleomoth's long, feathery antennae are good for picking up scents.

MOTH FACTS

- Most moths fly at night when the air is cold, so many of them have fat, hairy bodies to keep the warmth in.

- The Asian vampire moth can pierce the skin of an animal to drink its blood.

- Some moths have no mouths. Instead of eating, they survive on energy they stored up as caterpillars.

- We taste food with our tongues. But moths taste with their feet.

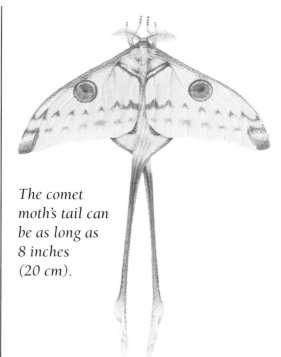

The comet moth's tail can be as long as 8 inches (20 cm).

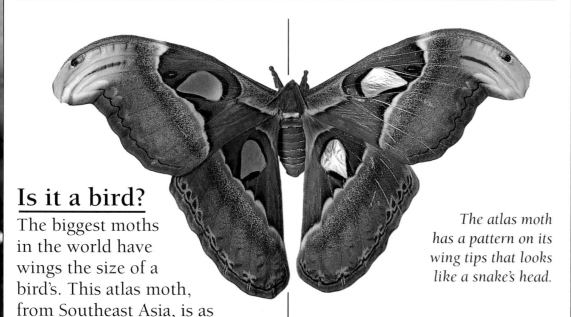

The atlas moth has a pattern on its wing tips that looks like a snake's head.

Is it a bird?

The biggest moths in the world have wings the size of a bird's. This atlas moth, from Southeast Asia, is as big as a blackbird. It stretches 12 inches (30 cm) from wing tip to wing tip. Even its caterpillars are about twice as long as your middle finger.

How much lunch can a caterpillar munch?

From the moment they are born, caterpillars spend their time stuffing themselves. These little eating machines have only one aim – to grow big enough to turn themselves into moths.

Do moths taste good?

The black and red colors on the wings of the cinnabar moth (below) warn birds that it tastes terrible. The moth's body is so tough that it is rarely hurt even if a bird does peck at it. But the bird gets a mouthful of bad-tasting liquid and flies off.

Do moths need tails?

Lots of moths have tails on their wings to disguise their shape. The comet moth (above) has one of the longest tails. Its head is well hidden, so any bird that spots it will probably peck at the trailing tail, giving the moth a chance to escape.

Can moths hear?

Some moths have an eardrum on each side of their body, which they use to listen for the high-pitched squeaks of a bat as it homes in on them in the dark. This advance warning gives the moths a few seconds to get out of the bat's way.

What is a butterfly?

BUTTERFLIES ARE INSECTS, closely related to moths. They fly by day, while most moths fly at night. And when they rest, most butterflies fold their wings over their backs. Moths hold their wings out flat.

How many wings do butterflies have?

Butterflies have four wings – two in front and two at the back. The wings look delicate but in fact are very strong.

A butterfly rolls up its proboscis when it is not feeding.

Front wing

Back wing

What is a chrysalis?

A chrysalis (right) is the halfway stage between a caterpillar and a butterfly. The caterpillar spins a silk cocoon to protect itself. While the caterpillar is in the cocoon, changing its shape, it is called a chrysalis. The butterfly that eventually climbs out of the cocoon has damp, crumpled wings. These must dry out before it can fly.

Which butterfly has eyes on its wings?

The owl butterfly (below) has huge eyespots on its wings. When it is at rest with its wings closed, it could easily be mistaken for a real owl.

How well can butterflies see?

Butterflies have two big, bulging compound eyes, made of hundreds of simple lenses. They see everything as a patchwork of tiny pictures.

Do butterflies fly far?

Every autumn, swarms of monarch butterflies migrate thousands of miles from North America to Mexico. They spend the winter in Mexico's warmer weather.

How big are butterflies?

The Queen Alexandra birdwing butterfly (above) is as big as a starling. The males are a beautiful bright blue. Collectors have killed so many of these butterflies that they are now protected by law.

How many eyes do caterpillars have?

Most caterpillars have twelve eyes, but their eyesight is poor. They can only tell the difference between light and dark. Some caterpillars have no eyes at all. They get around by touch and smell alone.

How do butterflies hide themselves?

The comma butterfly (below) hides from its enemies by staying still. It looks like a torn leaf on a twig, and the white "comma" in the middle of the back wing looks like a hole in the leaf.

Why do some butterflies like mud?

In hot countries, patches of damp earth attract large flocks of butterflies. They fly in to drink straight from the ground.

What do butterflies eat and drink?

Butterflies suck up the sweet nectar from flowers. They also drink dew and water from ponds or streams.

A butterfly's antennae have little knobs on the ends.

Where do butterflies sleep?

At night butterflies find a quiet place on a twig, a leaf, or a blade of grass. Often they sleep in the same place night after night because they know it is safe.

DID YOU KNOW?
The tiger butterfly on the right is poisonous, so birds don't touch it. Many other butterflies have the same colors and patterns, so they are safe from birds too.

BUTTERFLY FACTS

- Two butterflies may battle over a favorite patch of sunshine. Luckily they cannot hurt each other.

- Some butterflies sip the juices of rotten fruit. The juices contain alcohol, and sometimes a butterfly gets so drunk it can't fly.

- People often say "I have butterflies in my stomach" when they are worried and can feel their stomach fluttering.

What are frogs?

FROGS ARE AMPHIBIANS, as are toads, newts, and salamanders. Amphibians are animals that are born in water and spend the early part of their life there. Most don't learn to move on land until they are older.

Can a leaf croak?

You might think so, if you came across an Asian leaf frog (above). This little frog lives on the forest floor. Its brown skin, jagged shape, and hooded eyes make it look like a dead leaf.

What's for lunch?

This horned frog has an appetite to match the size of its mouth. It eats worms, insects, other frogs, rats – in fact, anything that it can fit!

The horned frog has no teeth, so it swallows its meals whole.

Which frogs have foamy feet?

Some tree frogs produce a liquid that they tread into a stiff foam with their feet. They lay their eggs in this foam, which dries to form a shell that protects the eggs while they develop.

Both the mole (a mammal) and the mole frog have wide, shovel-shaped front feet that are perfect for digging.

What are tadpoles?

Tadpoles (below) are baby frogs, although they don't look like frogs. They breathe through gills, like fish, and spend their time swimming and feeding on small plants and animals. After a while, little legs sprout, the tail shrinks, and the tadpole becomes a small frog.

Which frog looks like a mole?

The mole frog of Australia has a small molelike head with a rounded snout and tiny eyes. It digs headfirst, like a mole, and uses its strong front legs to sweep aside the sand as it hunts for insects.

Are frogs poisonous?

Some are. This tiny arrow-poison frog has a bright blue and black pattern to warn other animals that its skin is poisonous.

This red-eyed tree frog can leap right out of the water to catch a meal.

Are frogs fast movers?

Frogs move fast when it comes to grabbing a meal. They may sit still for a long time, waiting for an insect to come near. The moment it does, they leap at it like lightning and gulp it down.

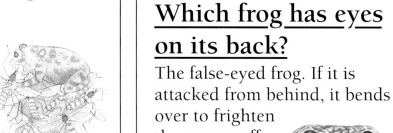

These White's tree frogs have sticky pads on their fingers and toes that help them cling to branches.

Are frogs friendly?

White's tree frog is quite happy to live on tree branches, but it often hops into people's homes, too. Once inside, it heads for cool, moist places, like sinks and bathtubs.

FROG FACTS

- The smallest frog is a cousin of the arrow-poison frogs. It is only about half an inch (8 to 12 mm) long.

- The glass frog has see-through skin. If you look closely, you can see its heart beating.

- A dwarf puddle frog is about the size of your thumb. But it can eat 100 mosquitoes in a single night.

- Some horned frogs have a croak that sounds like a cow mooing.

Which frog has eyes on its back?

The false-eyed frog. If it is attacked from behind, it bends over to frighten the enemy off with its two huge eyespots.

To keep their skin moist, tree frogs stay out of the sun as much as possible.

Can frogs climb?

Some tree frogs are such good climbers they spend their entire life up in the trees. These frogs eat, sleep, and lay their eggs among branches and leaves, so they never need to come down to the ground.

Do frogs eat eggs?

The Australian stomach-brooding frog swallows her eggs. The eggs develop inside her stomach and jump out of her mouth when they have grown into tiny frogs.

Are toads frogs?

TOADS AND FROGS ARE closely related, as you might guess from the way they look. But they are not the same. Toads have dry, warty skin, and frogs have smooth, moist skin. And frogs are much better at jumping and leaping than toads.

Are toads tasty?

Many toads have poison glands in special lumps behind their eyes. If a dog or another animal grabs the toad, it gets a squirt of foul-tasting liquid in its mouth and drops the toad at once.

This green toad feeds on insects. It catches them by flicking out its sticky tongue and dragging them into its mouth.

Do snakes eat toads?

Snakes don't mind the poison that toads produce. So toads have to find another way of defending themselves. Many puff up their body and stand on their toes to make themselves look too big to swallow.

Why do toads dig burrows?

Many toads hide from their enemies during the day by digging down into the ground. They burrow into loose soil with their hind feet and snuggle in backward. The cool, moist soil stops their skin from drying out in hot weather.

This little toad's coloring is a good disguise on the forest floor.

When do toads eat?

Most toads sleep during the day and hunt at night. They eat all kinds of animals, as long as they can fit them into their mouths. You will often see toads near lamps or other lights. They snap up insects that are attracted by the light.

DID YOU KNOW?
Animals are sometimes given the wrong names. The horned toad looks like a toad, but it is really a lizard. Toads do not have tails.

How big is a cane toad?

The cane toad (above) is about the size of a dinner plate. It is one of the largest toads in the world. The cane toad eats just about anything smaller than itself, including mice, beetles, crickets, and worms.

Do toads jump well?

Toads cannot jump as well as frogs. Many frogs can jump several times the length of their body. But this common toad, like most others, gets around by taking little hops.

Where do toads keep their eggs?

Most toads lay their eggs in pools of water, and leave them there. But the female Surinam toad lives under water and keeps her eggs in chambers in the spongy skin on her back until they turn into tiny toads.

DID YOU KNOW?
The holy cross toad uses the shovel on its back feet to bury itself eye-deep in soil. There it waits in hiding for a meal to come close enough to snatch.

Are toads useful?

Most toads stuff as much food into their mouths as they can. For this reason, many farmers and gardeners use them to keep the number of insects down. In Hawaii toads have been used to control the number of beetles damaging the sugarcane crop.

Why are two colors better than one?

The Oriental fire-bellied toad's green back hides it well in the forest. But if an enemy attacks, it flashes its bright red belly. Most animals know that bright colors mean poison.

Who looks after a midwife's babies?

The female midwife toad lays her eggs on the male's hind legs. He carries them around while they are developing, then he takes them to a pond, where the tadpoles hatch and swim free.

TOAD FACTS

- The smallest toad in the world is from Mozambique. It grows no bigger than 1 inch (24 mm) long.

- The spadefoot toad gets its name from its feet, which are perfectly shaped for digging.

- Toads and frogs are very noisy. The mating calls of some can be heard more than half a mile (1 km) away.

- Some toads can absorb water through the skin of their belly just by sitting on damp ground.

Why do birds sing?

BIRDS SING FOR ALL KINDS of reasons. Sometimes they want to attract a mate. Sometimes they want to warn other birds to stay away. In areas where there are many birds, and they all sing in a dawn chorus, the sound can be very loud!

With its long beak, the hummingbird can reach deep inside flowers for nectar.

When do birds hum?

Hummingbirds hover next to a flower while they feed. They have to beat their wings up to 70 times a second – so fast that you can hardly see them. But you can hear the humming sound the beating wings make.

What does an oxpecker peck?

Oxpeckers eat the ticks and flies that bother many large animals living on the plains of Africa. So the animals let these birds walk all over them, pecking up the pests.

How do pelicans fish?

When a pelican spots a fish below the surface, it dives straight toward the fish and opens its beak wide. Its throat pouch swells to trap the fish like a net.

The water that rushes into a pelican's beak with the fish can weigh more than the bird.

When do male frigatebirds go red?

When they see a female frigatebird. The male has a red pouch at his throat that he can blow up like a balloon. The bigger and redder it is, the more attractive he is to a female.

Do wagtails hunt?

The wagtail (below) lives by streams and lakes. It waits on a rock or bank, and darts out over the water to snap up passing insects with its long, pointed beak.

Why should a home have two doors?

The Cape penduline tit (above) builds its nest with a false entrance so enemies think there is no way in. The real entrance is smaller and easy to miss.

What makes a bird's hair stand on end?

Many cockatoos make the tuft of feathers at the back of their head stand on end when they become excited or angry. They do this to warn off other birds.

When does a peacock walk backward?

When he is trying to charm a peahen. He opens his train of dazzling feathers with his back to her, then walks closer and closer. At last he whirls around and displays the train in all its glory.

Which crane has a crown?

The black crowned crane's head is topped with straw-colored feathers that look like a crown. But it is the black feathers at the front that give this bird its name.

The black crowned crane can grow to 3 feet (1 m) tall.

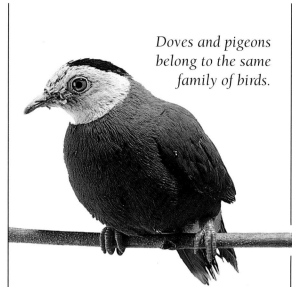

Doves and pigeons belong to the same family of birds.

How can flamingos eat upside down?

The flamingo lowers its beak upside down into the water to trap tiny plants and shrimp. The bird's swallowing muscles are so strong that it can gulp up fish without raising its head.

How does a dove drink?

Doves have pointed beaks for feeding on seeds and leaves. They also use their beak like a straw, to suck up water.

Where do emperors keep their eggs?

Emperor penguins live in Antarctica. The female goes off to feed as soon as she has laid the egg, which the male keeps warm by carrying on his feet. After the chick has hatched, it stays warm in the same way.

BIRD FACTS

- The most common bird is the seed-eating quelea of Africa. There are about 10 billion queleas.

- All birds have four toes. The arrangement of the toes tells us whether the bird is best at perching, climbing, or paddling.

- The kea of southern New Zealand often hangs around ski resorts, where it rolls around and plays in the snow.

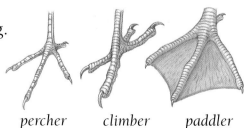

percher　　*climber*　　*paddler*

Are birds dangerous?

BIRDS OF PREY ARE DANGEROUS, but only to small or medium-sized animals. These meat eaters have long claws for stabbing and gripping their prey and sharp, powerful beaks for tearing it apart. Some may fly hundreds of miles each day in search of a meal.

The eagle's high nest gives it a good view so it can look for other birds.

Whose nest looks like an unmade bed?

An eagle piles big sticks in a heap to make a nest. The nest looks messy, but it's strong and lasts for several years. Eagles build their nests at the top of dead trees, so the eggs are fairly safe.

*DID YOU KNOW?
Birds of prey can see about four times as well as people. Some hawks can spot a grasshopper 300 feet (100 m) away.*

Which bird makes a big splash?

With its wings folded back and its feet forward, an osprey hits the water and vanishes in a fountain of spray. If it has aimed well, it will rise into the air with a fish held firmly in its claws.

How do owls hunt in the dark?

Owls could probably hunt blindfolded. They can hear the slightest rustle of feet and home in on a target by their hearing alone. But owls have good eyesight, too, and can see clearly even on dark nights.

The Egyptian vulture is one of the few birds known to use tools.

Do birds eat eggs?

Egyptian vultures don't even wait for their prey to hatch. These vultures love to eat the eggs of other large birds, such as ostriches. They use rocks as tools, throwing the rocks at the eggs to smash the shells.

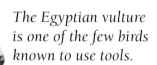

Who likes fast food?

Peregrine falcons hunt mostly other birds. They dive at their prey from above, tucking their wings back to gain extra speed. The prey falls to the ground when it is hit, and the falcon follows to snatch up its prize.

What do eagles eat?

Most eagles hunt animals small enough to pick up and carry away. But if they manage to kill a larger animal, they eat it on the spot. Eagles kill with their claws and use their sharp beaks to cut through the flesh.

A secretary bird has longer legs than any other bird of prey.

Do secretaries dance?

When a secretary bird is looking for a mate, it does a little dance on the ground and makes fabulous swoops and dives in the air.

Which is the heaviest bird of prey?

The Andean condor is the heaviest bird of prey. It weighs up to 25 pounds (12 kg). Condors are weak fliers, and rain soon grounds them. They have to spread their wings out to dry before they can take off.

What does a harpy eagle hunt?

The mighty harpy eagle can chase a monkey through the treetops at up to 45 miles per hour (70 km/h). It also plucks sloths, snakes, and opossums out of the branches.

BIRD OF PREY FACTS

- Vultures hunt during the heat of the day when they can save energy by gliding on warm air currents, called thermals.

- One eye is set higher on an owl's head than the other. The owl sees two different images, which helps it figure out how far the object is.

- Up to 100 vultures at a time may feed on the carcass (dead body) of one animal. If there is more than enough food, these birds sometimes eat so much that they can't fly.

What is a snake?

SNAKES ARE REPTILES that have no hands or feet. They move by wriggling or creeping. A snake is mostly backbone, with a head at one end and a whiplike tail at the other. Many snakes have a poisonous bite.

Can snakes catch birds?

The tree boa (above) can catch birds on the wing. It waits in a tree until a bird flies by, then flings itself straight at its victim, wraps around it, and squeezes it to death.

This milk snake (left) has the same coloring as the venomous coral snake. But you can tell them apart by the pattern.

Why is a vine snake green?

The vine snake (below) lives in trees. Its green skin blends in with the color of the trees, making it difficult to see.

Do milk snakes drink milk?

They never touch the stuff! They hang around cowsheds only because of the mice that live there. Milk snakes kill their victims by squeezing. Then they swallow them whole.

If a cobra is alarmed, it rears up, spreads the hood of skin on the sides of its neck, and hisses.

Do rattlesnakes make friends?

Not really. Rattlesnakes spend most of their time alone. In winter, however, they gather in large groups to sleep through the cold weather. Sometimes as many as 1,000 snakes will hole up together in a single den. This helps them to stay warm.

Why don't desert snakes get burned?

They would if they crawled through the hot sand. Instead they move by "side-winding." They arch their bodies from side to side and hardly touch the ground.

DID YOU KNOW?
It's not the snake charmer's music that makes a cobra dance and sway. The fact is, a cobra is almost deaf. Although it seems to be following the music, all it's really doing is following the pipe as the charmer waves it slowly back and forth.

Baby snakes have a special egg tooth for breaking out of their eggshell.

Is a baby cobra dangerous?

A cobra is deadly from the moment it hatches. Like most snakes, cobras lay eggs and then leave them to hatch. As soon as a baby cobra is out of the egg, it has to look after itself. That means attacking and killing other animals to get a meal.

SNAKE FACTS

- Snakes stick out their tongues to smell what is in the air.

- Some snakes live in the sea. Their bite can kill a fish in seconds.

- The black mamba is one of the fastest snakes on the ground. It can move at nearly 7 miles per hour (11 km/h) – a bit faster than you can walk.

Can snakes fly?

No snake can fly, but there is one that can glide. It lives in the jungles of Asia and launches itself from the tops of trees. As it glides through the air on flaps of skin along the sides of its body, it steers by twisting from side to side.

Flying snakes flatten and widen their bodies for gliding.

Egg-eating snakes coil their body around an egg to hold it steady.

DID YOU KNOW?
Egg-eating snakes can gulp down eggs twice as big as their head. Their mouth stretches like rubber to take in the egg. Their jaws are flexible too – the lower jaw can unhook from the upper one.

Can snakes hunt at night?

Many snakes can see better at night than they can in daylight, and some, like this tree boa, have an extra sense. Through tiny holes around its lips, it can feel the body heat of its prey.

How do you milk a snake?

Snakes don't produce milk. But some produce a venom, or poison, that we use in medicines. People collect the venom by gently squeezing the back of a snake's head.

Do crocodiles cry?

CROCODILES APPEAR TO CRY when they eat, and so they look as though they are feeling sorry for their prey. But a crocodile's tears are really just a way of getting rid of all the salt from the water that the animal swallows with its food. This is why people often use the phrase "crocodile tears" to mean fake tears!

How do crocs hatch?

Like most reptiles, baby crocodiles have an egg tooth to help them break out of the egg. But if they have difficulty, Mom can help crack the shell.

What do crocs eat?

Baby crocodiles eat insects. As they grow, they catch larger animals, such as frogs and fish. Fully grown crocodiles eat deer, antelopes – even zebras.

Crocodiles, alligators, caimans, and gavials all belong to the same family.

DID YOU KNOW? In ancient Egypt, people showed their respect for the Nile crocodile by giving their god Sebek a crocodile head in all the pictures and statues that they made of him.

Do crocodiles clean their teeth?

They don't have to – a plover like this one will do it for them. The crocodile lets the bird pick its teeth for scraps of leftover food. Having clean teeth may be good for the crocodile too.

What is a gavial?

The gavial (above) is a cousin of the crocodile. It lives in rivers in northern India. A gavial has a long, slender snout full of dagger-like teeth, which it uses to catch fish.

Crocodiles yawn when they're hot, not when they're tired.

Do crocodiles yawn?

Yes, but not because they are tired. When they bask in the sun, they get hot. So they open their jaws wide to help them cool down. A crocodile can lose heat quickly from the inside of its mouth.

How do caimans hide?

The caiman (above), like all crocodiles and alligators, has its eyes and nose on the top of its head, so it can see and breathe when most of its body is under water. It glides slowly up to its prey, then suddenly attacks.

Can crocodiles jump?

Only in water. They use their strong, flattened tails to push themselves out of the water so they can grab animals from overhanging branches. They can swim fast, too. But on land crocodiles are clumsy animals.

An alligator's eyes are on the top of its head.

Can crocodiles chew?

Crocodile teeth are perfect for grabbing and holding prey but not for chewing. A crocodile usually drags prey into the water and holds it under until it drowns. Then it tears off chunks of flesh and swallows them whole.

Why do crocodiles swallow stones?

Scientists have found stones in the stomachs of crocodiles and alligators. The stones may have been swallowed on purpose, to help them grind up food.

Do crocs make nests?

Many crocodiles make nests for their eggs. The mother guards the eggs, but when they hatch, she carries her babies gently to the water and leaves them to take care of themselves.

CROCODILE FACTS

- Crocodiles often lose teeth, but new ones grow quickly. A crocodile can have more than fifty complete sets of teeth in a lifetime.

- Estuarine crocodiles are the biggest of all. They can grow up to 27 feet (8 m) long.

- When an alligator dives, it clamps its nostrils shut and closes its ear tubes. A flap at the back of its throat stops water from getting into its lungs.

Do dragons exist?

NO ONE HAS EVER FOUND PROOF of flying, fire-breathing dragons like those of legend. But take one look at a lizard and you will see where people got the idea!

A gecko can't blink, so it wipes its eyes with its tongue instead.

When do lizards lose their tails?

When they are in serious danger, many lizards have a great trick. If an enemy catches a lizard by the tail, the tail breaks off. The tail keeps wriggling while the lizard runs off to live another day.

Do geckos bark?

Geckos are little lizards that can click, chirp, and bark. They use these noises when courting a mate or defending their home. Very few reptiles can make this many different sounds.

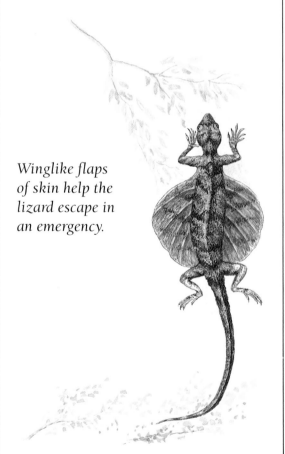

Winglike flaps of skin help the lizard escape in an emergency.

Are frills useful?

They are to a frilled lizard. It runs from danger when it can. But if it is cornered, the lizard hisses and raises its frill like a huge collar. This scares off most enemies, even though the lizard is actually harmless.

DID YOU KNOW?
Some lizards, such as the glass lizard (below), have no legs at all. They slink about like snakes or burrow like worms.

How do chameleons change color?

A chameleon's skin cells contain color substances called pigments. When the cells get bigger or smaller, the skin color changes. No one knows what controls the cells.

Can lizards fly?

Flying lizards can't really fly – they don't have wings. But they can make long, controlled downward glides using flaps of skin that open out along the sides of their body.

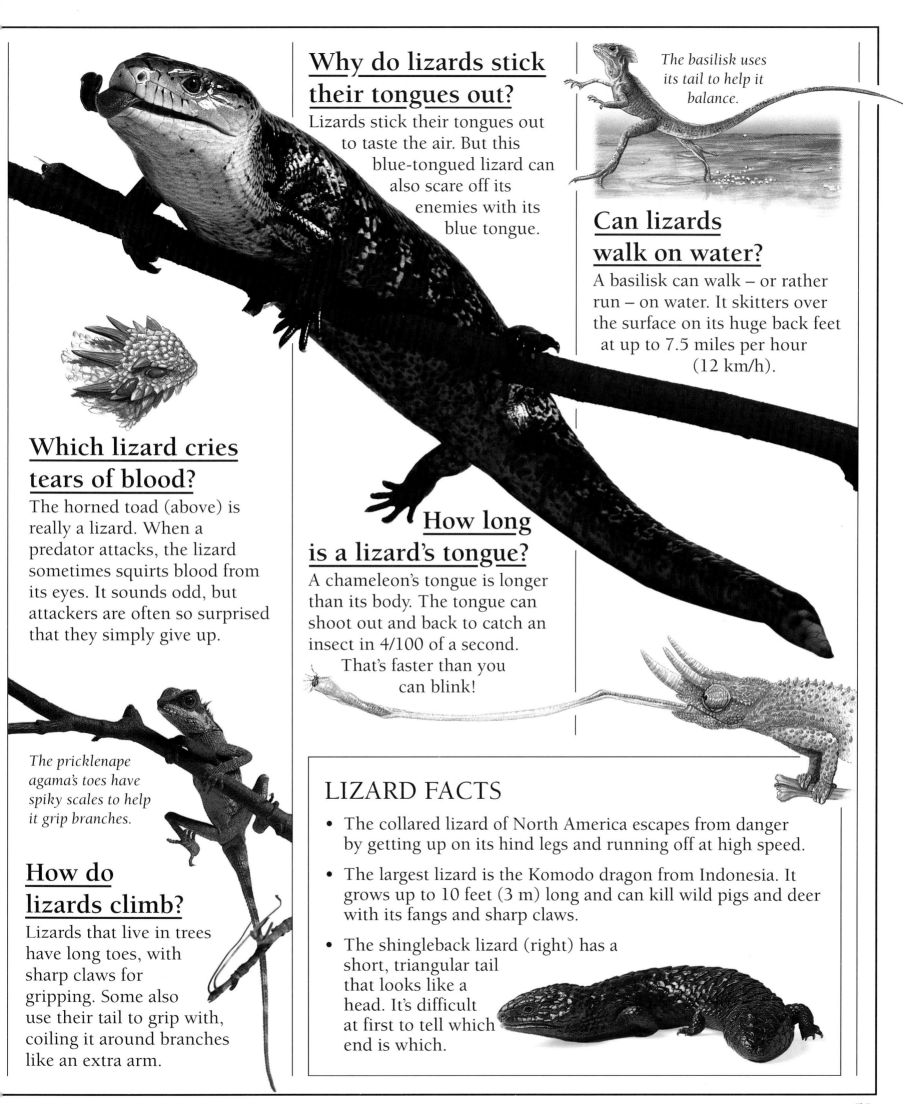

Why do lizards stick their tongues out?

Lizards stick their tongues out to taste the air. But this blue-tongued lizard can also scare off its enemies with its blue tongue.

The basilisk uses its tail to help it balance.

Can lizards walk on water?

A basilisk can walk – or rather run – on water. It skitters over the surface on its huge back feet at up to 7.5 miles per hour (12 km/h).

Which lizard cries tears of blood?

The horned toad (above) is really a lizard. When a predator attacks, the lizard sometimes squirts blood from its eyes. It sounds odd, but attackers are often so surprised that they simply give up.

How long is a lizard's tongue?

A chameleon's tongue is longer than its body. The tongue can shoot out and back to catch an insect in 4/100 of a second. That's faster than you can blink!

The pricklenape agama's toes have spiky scales to help it grip branches.

How do lizards climb?

Lizards that live in trees have long toes, with sharp claws for gripping. Some also use their tail to grip with, coiling it around branches like an extra arm.

LIZARD FACTS

- The collared lizard of North America escapes from danger by getting up on its hind legs and running off at high speed.

- The largest lizard is the Komodo dragon from Indonesia. It grows up to 10 feet (3 m) long and can kill wild pigs and deer with its fangs and sharp claws.

- The shingleback lizard (right) has a short, triangular tail that looks like a head. It's difficult at first to tell which end is which.

Who lives in a box?

TORTOISES AND TURTLES live inside a thick shell that covers their body like a suit of armor. Only the head, legs, and tail stick out. If danger threatens, tortoises and turtles can pull these inside, too.

What is a terrapin?

A terrapin is a freshwater turtle. It eats plants, worms, carrion (dead animals), and anything else it can find. People often keep terrapins as pets, but they usually die of malnutrition before they are fully grown.

Do turtles smell bad?

There is a small turtle in North America that can make a very unpleasant smell. It's called a stinkpot turtle. When a bird or other animal picks it up, it releases the scent. Usually the enemy drops the turtle at once.

DID YOU KNOW?
Depending on where they live, turtles and tortoises have differently shaped feet.

land   sea   fresh water

DID YOU KNOW?
The leatherback turtle (below) spends most of its life at sea. It comes ashore only to lay eggs.

Why do turtles snap?

The snapping turtle (right) lurks at the bottom of rivers or ponds, snapping up fish as they swim by. Some snapping turtles even attack human hands or feet!

How do turtles fish?

The alligator snapper (below) sits on the bottom of a swamp or a creek and holds its mouth open. When a curious fish comes along to look at a bright pink, wriggling worm, the turtle's powerful jaws snap it up. The worm is really a part of the snapper's tongue.

This little fish is about to have a nasty surprise.

Why do turtles cry?

Marine (sea-living) turtles swallow seawater as they feed. Too much salt is bad for them, so, like crocodiles, they cry salty tears to get rid of it.

What shape is a tortoise's shell?

Giant tortoises that live on islands where food plants grow on the ground have a gently curved shell. Those on islands where food grows higher up have a groove at the front of their shell so they can raise their heads.

What if a shell is too small for you?

A turtle with a small shell has a real problem. The big-headed turtle (right) has a head that is far too big to pull into its shell. Luckily, the head is covered in extra tough skin.

Can shells bend?

The hingeback tortoise (above) can swing part of its shell down at the back to protect the rear of its body. Then it nudges the front of its shell against a rock to guard its head.

Giant tortoises have been known to live for more than a century.

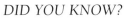

DID YOU KNOW?
A fully grown giant tortoise can be 3 feet (1 m) long and weigh nearly as much as three people. But a fully grown leatherback turtle is as heavy as a small car, and its flippers span about 12 feet (3.5 m).

Can a shell be a door?

Gopher tortoises share their homes with frogs and mice, but they can keep out snakes by using their shell as a door.

TURTLE FACTS

- Many river turtles soak up oxygen through their skin. They can stay under water for days without coming up for air.

- Green turtles feed along the coast of South America, but they travel 1,367 miles (2,200 km) across the Atlantic to lay their eggs on Ascension Island.

- Before turtles go in search of food, they warm up by basking in the sun for hours.

Do fish breathe air?

FISH CAN'T BREATHE AIR because they don't have lungs. Instead they have gills, which they use to take oxygen from the water. You can tell their gills are working by watching the flaps behind their head – the flaps open and close as water flows past.

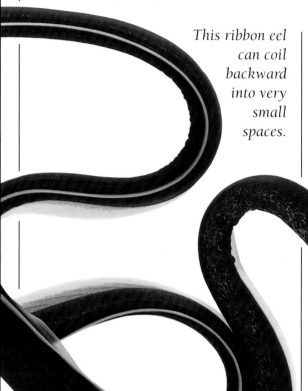

This ribbon eel can coil backward into very small spaces.

How do eels get meals?

They smell them. Eels have a better sense of smell than any other fish. By day they hide in caves, or nooks and crannies along rocky coasts. At night they come out to hunt for food.

This ribbon eel is a kind of moray eel. Moray eels often hide in a crevice with only their heads sticking out, waiting for prey to swim past.

Do fish lay eggs?

Some fish lay hundreds of eggs, which drift about in the sea and are gobbled up by all kinds of hungry animals. Other fish lay fewer eggs and keep them in a nest where they can watch over them. These eggs have a better chance of hatching without being eaten.

Which eels live in gardens?

Garden eels live in groups, with their tails buried in the sand and their heads pointed into the current. A crowd of them looks like a patch of tall grass.

How does a filefish hide?

The filefish (left) has a clever trick for avoiding enemies. It hides in the seaweed and sways gently in the current, just like a piece of seaweed. From the front, the fish is so thin it is almost invisible.

When the porcupine fish is full of air or water, its sharp spines stick out.

Which fish blows itself up?

When a porcupine fish is in danger, it puffs itself up by swallowing water or air. This makes the fish far too big for other fish to swallow.

Can dads give birth?

Male sea horses have a pouch on their belly, in which the female lays her eggs. Then she swims off, leaving Dad to look after them. When the young hatch, they pop out of their father's pouch.

How can a stone kill?

Stonefish look just like stones on the seabed. But watch your step – the spines on their fins have a poison that can kill a human in less than two hours.

Do fish sleep?

Fish sleep with their eyes open because they have no eyelids. But they can shut their pupils. This dogfish has narrowed its pupil to let in less light while it snoozes.

Would you eat a deadly fish?

Japanese people try to cut out the poisonous parts of *fugu*, or the death pufferfish, before they eat it. But *fugu* still causes about twenty deaths every year.

FISH FACTS

- A fully grown electric eel can give off a shock powerful enough to light up a whole house.

- Most fish are protected by a layer of hard, thin scales. A few, such as the catfish, have no scales at all.

- Some fish are so well adapted to living at the bottom of the sea that if they come to the surface too quickly, they pop!

Can fish fish?

The anglerfish (above) can. It sits on a reef with its tongue out. The tongue looks like a juicy worm. When a fish swims by, the angler opens its huge mouth and sucks the fish in.

This viperfish attracts prey in the darkness of the deep sea by producing its own light.

Which fish has extra teeth?

The deep-sea viperfish attacks fish bigger than itself. Its jaws can swing wide open like a door. Inside the mouth, long teeth curve backward to keep prey from escaping, and extra teeth in the throat grip the meal and help push it down toward the fish's huge stomach.

What do sharks eat?

YOU MAY HAVE HEARD STORIES of sharks eating people, but most sharks eat much smaller prey, which is easier to catch. Some sharks feed on plankton (microscopic plants and animals); some eat fish; some eat other sharks and their cousins, the rays. Sharks rarely eat humans.

Most sharks have a streamlined shape, like this spinner shark.

What's great, white, and deadly?

The great white shark has a reputation for killing people. Its jaws are 300 times as powerful as yours, and its razor-sharp teeth are as long as your fingers. This fearsome shark feeds mostly on fish, seals, and other sharks, and seldom attacks people.

How do sharks trick fish?

The spinner shark (above) has a neat trick to fool its prey. It charges into a school of fish, then suddenly begins to spin around. Fish trying to escape have no idea which way the shark is headed.

What are rays?

Rays are closely related to sharks, and like sharks they have skeletons made of flexible cartilage instead of hard bones. Rays have flat bodies, well suited to feeding on the bottom of the sea.

Which shark lashes its prey with its tail?

A thresher shark's tail is as long as its body. It lashes its tail in the water to herd fish into a tight group. Then the shark slices through the group, gulping all the fish it can.

Which shark looks like seaweed?

The Australian wobbegong (above) lies on the seabed waiting for its prey. Fish and crabs often mistake it for seaweed and swim up to its jaws.

Can rays fly?

As it flaps its huge wings up and down, the manta ray (below) seems to be flying under water. Mantas sometimes leap right out of the water, then fall back with a big splash!

How do sharks find lunch?

Most sharks have an amazing sense of smell. They could smell a single drop of blood mixed in a bathtub full of water. Sharks also have pits next to their eyes, that can feel the ripples of electricity that fish make as they swim about.

You can see why the hammerhead shark got its name.

What does a hammerhead eat?

Hammerhead sharks eat fish, such as catfish and rays. Many rays have poisonous spines on their tails that protect them from most predators. But the spines don't seem to bother hammerheads.

Epaulette sharks grow to about 3 feet (1 m) long.

Can sharks walk?

The epaulette shark, like many small sharks, feeds on the seabed. It uses its side fins like legs to walk along as it searches for sea urchins, crabs, small fish, and other food.

Do sharks like blood?

Sharks don't mind blood at all. In fact, a bleeding fish or other animal draws them like a magnet. As they rush to feed, they often get so excited that they bite anything that moves, including each other.

DID YOU KNOW?
Sharks live mostly at sea, but some kinds swim up rivers from time to time. Bull sharks have been found hundreds of miles up the Amazon River in South America.

This eagle ray looks as graceful as a bird as it swims through the water on its broad, flat wings.

Are rays dangerous?

Most rays are harmless to humans. But stingrays have poisonous spines on their tails to defend themselves against anything that comes too close. The spines are connected to poison sacs, and they are very painful if they touch you as you swim past.

SHARK & RAY FACTS

- Sharks are constantly losing teeth and growing new ones. They may go through more than 20,000 teeth during a lifetime.

- The Atlantic torpedo ray can stun its prey with more than 200 volts of electricity. 200 volts could almost run a television set!

- The largest shark, the whale shark, can grow up to 60 feet (18 m) long.

Where do crabs live?

CRABS, LOBSTERS, SHRIMPS, wood lice, and barnacles belong to the group of animals called crustaceans. Most crustaceans live in the sea, but some prefer fresh water, and a few have even adapted to life on land.

Male lobsters have much bigger claws than female lobsters.

This arrowhead crab's legs can reach much farther sideways than they can reach forward.

Do crabs always walk sideways?

Many crabs can go forward, backward, and sideways. But their legs are close together, and they can take only small steps forward or backward. They can take bigger steps and run faster sideways.

Which "spider" has two extra legs?

Spiders have eight legs. But spider crabs, like all crabs, have ten. Two legs have pincers on the ends, used to grab and hold food. The other legs are for walking and running.

Where do lobsters hide?

Lobsters spend most of their time in rocky nooks and crannies. Their favorite hideout is a sandy hole under a rock. Once they have dug a hole just the right shape, lobsters come out only to find food.

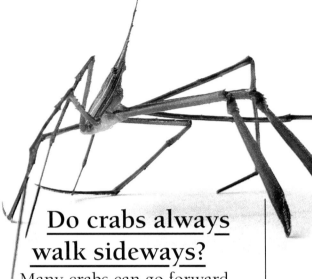

Which crabs have urchin friends?

The Adam's urchin crab (above) clings to a sea urchin for safety. The striped patterns on the crab's back and legs blend with the urchin's spines, and most predators avoid sea urchins because of their sting. This means the crab is safe too.

Spiny spider crabs are among the largest crabs.

Which shrimp is a giant?

The mantis shrimp (above) is three times the size of most other shrimps. It lives in shallow water, not far from sandy shores, and crushes its prey with its spiny front claws.

This decorator crab covers itself with pieces of plant and sponge from the seabed. Tiny bristles hold the pieces in place.

When do lobsters travel in trains?

When spiny lobsters (below) migrate to deeper water to lay eggs, they travel in long trains, often hanging on to the one in front. They sometimes travel nearly 100 miles (150 km) in this way.

Do hermit crabs move house?

Hermit crabs don't have their own shells, so they look for empty snail or whelk shells to live in. You can't often tempt a hermit crab out of its home, but when it finds a better shell, it scuttles rapidly out of its old home and into the new one.

What do crabs eat?

Crabs aren't the slightest bit fussy about what they eat. They nibble all the leftovers they can find on the bottom of the sea. They also catch fish and worms, and crunch up other kinds of small animals with their pincers.

Crayfish look a lot like their cousins, the lobsters.

Why are crabs like medieval knights?

Crabs, like medieval knights, wear armor that's tough enough to protect them. And a crab's shell is jointed, just like armor. But unlike knights, crabs can take their armor off only when they molt.

Is a crayfish a fish?

Many animals with the word fish in their name are not fish at all, including shellfish, crayfish (below), and cuttlefish. Crayfish are freshwater relatives of lobsters. They live under stones or in burrows in streams and ponds.

CRAB FACTS

- The pea crab has a smooth, round body no bigger than a pea. It lives inside the shells of mussels and clams.

- The robber crab spends most of its time on land. It is said to feed on coconuts, climbing up palm trees like a monkey and snipping the stalks of the coconuts with its claws.

- The giant Japanese spider crab is the biggest crab in the world. It can grow to up to 10 feet (3 m) from leg tip to leg tip. That's farther than you can jump!

INDEX

GLOSSARY

amphibians *animals that live both on land and in water, such as frogs and toads*

arachnids *animals with simple eyes and eight legs, such as spiders, scorpions, and ticks*

blubber *the layer of fat just under the skin of a mammal, such as a walrus, that keeps it warm*

camouflage *colors and patterns that match an animal's surroundings and help disguise it*

carcass *the dead body of an animal*

carrion *the flesh of a dead animal*

cold-blooded animals *animals that need the sun to keep their bodies warm*

constricting *squeezing to death, a method some snakes use to kill their prey*

fertile *able to produce young*

gills *the organs that some animals, such as fish, use for taking in oxygen from water*

hibernation *a sleep that lasts through winter*

larvae *the grub-like young of some insects, which will develop into adults*

loping *slow running with a long stride, as wolves do, to cover long distances*

malnutrition *lack of nourishment, caused by an unbalanced diet*

mammals *animals that have warm blood and feed milk to their young*

mantle *the part of a mollusk that makes the shell*

marine *sea-living*

mollusk *a soft-bodied animal, such as a snail, that often has a shell*

operculum *a protective cover, such as the disk on a snail's foot that blocks the entrance to its shell*

parasite *an animal or plant that lives on another*

plankton *tiny, floating sea animals and plants*

prey *an animal hunted for food*

prehensile tails *tails that can grasp*

primates *advanced mammals, such as apes, monkeys, and humans*

reptiles *cold-blooded animals, such as tortoises, snakes, lizards, and crocodiles*

siphon *the tube that an octopus has for breathing, feeding, and moving*

thermals *warm currents in the air which some birds, such as vultures, use to help them glide*

underfur *the thick fur next to the skin of some animals that helps keep them warm*

warm-blooded animals *animals whose body temperature is always the same*

ACKNOWLEDGMENTS

**Dorling Kindersley would like to thank
the following for their photographs:**

Jane Burton, Geoff Dann, Mike Dunning, Frank Greenaway,
Colin Keates, Dave King, Karl Shone, Kim Taylor, Jerry Young

and the following for their illustrations:
Julie Anderson, John Bendall-Brunello, Ruth Benton,
John Davis, Angelika Elsbach, Gill Elsbury, Jane Gedye,
John Hutchinson, Mark Iley, Ruth Lindsay, Polly Noakes,
Valerie Price, Colin Woolf, Dan Wright